MW01182171

spy, n. — a secret agent employed by a government or other organization
to gather intelligence relating to its actual or potential enemies

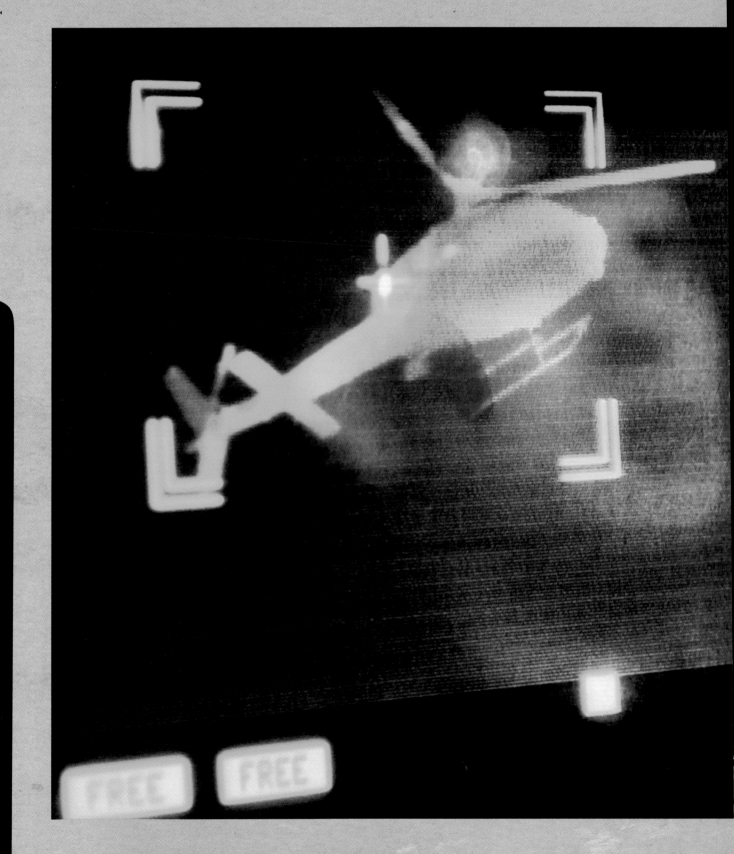

Spies around the World

SIS

AND OTHER BRITISH SPIES

Michael E. Goodman

CREATIVE EDUCATION

In the 1960s, British spies kept a close eye on Soviet Union ships in Atlantic waters.

Table of Contents

Chapters

- -

Evolution of Espionage

- -

Published by Creative Education
P.O. Box 227, Mankato, Minnesota 56002
Creative Education is an imprint of
The Creative Company
www.thecreativecompany.us

Design and production by Blue Design
Art direction by Rita Marshall
Printed in the United States of America

Photographs by by Getty Images (AFP, Margaret Bourke-
White//Time Life Pictures, Central Press, Central
Press/Hulton Archive, Martin Cleaver/Pool, CARL
COURT/AFP, Tony Evans, Hulton Archive, Images of
Empire/Universal Images Group, Keystone, John Li,
Peter Macdiarmid, John Moore, Suzanne Plunkett/
Bloomberg, Paul Popper/Popperfoto, Popperfoto,
SSPL, D. Thiel/Express, Time Life Pictures/National
Archives/Time Life Pictures, United Artists,
Universal History Archive, KIRSTY WIGGLESWORTH/AFP,
Greg Williams/Eon Productions)

Library of Congress Cataloging-in-Publication Data
Goodman, Michael E.
The SIS and other British spies / by Michael E.
Goodman.
p. cm.   (Spies around the world)
Includes bibliographical references and index.
Summary: An eye-opening exploration of the history
of the 1909-founded SIS and other British espionage
agencies, investigating their typical training and
tools as well as the escapades of famous spies.
ISBN 978-1-60818-229-9
1. Intelligence service Great Britain Juvenile
literature. 2. Great Britain. MI6 Juvenile
literature. 3. Espionage, British Juvenile
literature. 4. Spies Great Britain Juvenile
literature. I. Title.

JN329.I6G66 2012
327.1241 dc23   2011035791

CPSIA: 061313 PO1705
9 8 7 6 5 4 3 2

Early supercomputers helped other countries break German codes during World War II.

In 1939, a British spymaster convinced a bright
young man named Ian Fleming to join his group.
Fleming's job was to think of creative ways
of defeating the Germans during World War II
(1939 45). One of his ideas that came to fruition
involved using astrology to persuade a Nazi
leader to defect to England. Another which was
never implemented called for British soldiers
to dress up in German uniforms and take over
a German rescue boat to steal its code books.
After the war, Fleming turned his imagination
to writing about spies and evil masterminds. His
novels featured Britain's Secret Intelligence
Service (SIS) and a daring, dashing operative
named James Bond.

A CULTURE OF SECRECY

I n 1588, a powerful fleet of ships sailed north from Spain, intent on destroying the English navy and conquering England. The Spanish might have succeeded if their attack had been a surprise. Instead, a spy planted inside the Spanish king's court by the English secretary of state relayed vital intelligence about the attack. Thanks to that advance warning, the English navy was able to defeat the Spanish Armada. After that battle, England's fortunes increased around the world, and Spain's declined.

English rulers and government leaders from Queen Elizabeth I (1533–1603) to Queen Victoria (1819–1901) often used spies both inside and outside the country. Yet Great Britain did not have an official intelligence organization until 1909. That was the year that the Secret Service Bureau was established. It consisted of two main components: a Foreign Section to handle intelligence gathering and covert operations outside the country and a Home Section responsible for catching spies and fighting terrorism domestically. The more formal name

of Secret Intelligence Service was adopted for the Foreign Section in 1922. Later, it came to be called MI6, which is short for Military Intelligence Section 6. SIS employees often call it "The Firm." The Home Section was renamed the Security Service in 1931 and later became known as MI5, short for Military Intelligence Section 5. The SIS is similar to the Central Intelligence Agency (CIA) in the United States, while the Security Service is parallel to the Federal Bureau of Investigation (FBI).

The first head of the Foreign Section/SIS was Captain Mansfield Cumming, who served from 1909

until his death in 1923. Cumming instituted several SIS traditions that continue today. For example, he always signed his name with the initial "C." The letter stood for both "Cumming" and "Chief." All SIS chiefs since Cumming have also been called "C," no matter what their name has been. (In Ian Fleming's James Bond novels, the head of the SIS is similarly known as "M.") Cumming also used green ink for writing notes, and a bottle of green ink still sits atop the SIS chief's desk in London.

Cumming enforced a culture of strict secrecy on the SIS. Agents' names were never publicly revealed,

Right: The Spanish Armada was supposed to have paved the way for Catholicism to re-emerge as England's official religion.

EVOLUTION OF ESPIONAGE
Queen Elizabeth's Spymaster

The reign of Queen Elizabeth I (1558 1603) was filled with spying and intrigue. Because Elizabeth was Protestant, many European leaders who were Catholic wanted to overthrow her. Elizabeth appointed Sir Francis Walsingham as her secretary of state (a position then called principal secretary). Walsingham recruited and trained a group of ambitious college students to become spies, teaching them how to break codes and do undercover work. One time, Walsingham's spies learned of a plot to assassinate Elizabeth and put her Catholic cousin Mary, Queen of Scots, on the throne. They intercepted and decoded a message from Mary to one of the conspirators. The evidence of Mary's guilt led Elizabeth to order her cousin's execution.

not even if they died in service. Agents were also prohibited from telling others anything about their training, colleagues, or missions. That ban is still in effect today. In fact, revealing agency secrets is against British law, as one former agent, Richard Tomlinson, unfortunately discovered. Tomlinson was imprisoned in the late 1990s when he tried to publish a memoir of his experiences. (He later succeeded in his goal, thanks in large part to the Internet.)

Just five years after the Secret Service Bureau was formed, Europe entered World War I (1914–18). The Foreign Section joined with intelligence organizations from France, Italy, Russia, and the U.S. to monitor the movement of German troops during the war. It also established its first foreign offices in the Netherlands, France, Egypt, and America.

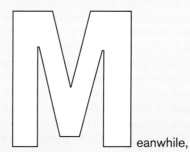 eanwhile, the Home Section focused on uncovering German spies operating inside England. Even though the section had only 14 employees at the time, it managed to identify and break up several active German spy rings. Its greatest triumph occurred on August 4, 1914, the same day that Great Britain declared war

on Germany, when British agents captured 21 German spies they had been tracking.

Following World War I, British intelligence efforts dealt primarily with threats posed to Europe by communist Russia, where a political and social revolution had taken place. Russia's new leaders had renamed their country the Soviet Union. Fearing that these leaders were planning to spread communism throughout Europe, the SIS sent two top agents into the Soviet Union. The agents hoped to assassinate Vladimir Lenin, the

The first assassination plot against the queen that Francis Walsingham helped uncover was in 1570.

Britain's Royal Air Force documented bombing sites and gathered intelligence in the 1940s.

leader of the communist revolution, but they were unsuccessful.

Paying so much attention to the Soviet Union distracted British intelligence from Adolf Hitler's rise to power within Germany's Nazi Party in the 1930s. As World War II loomed, two new organizations were established under SIS control. One was the Government Code and Cypher School (GC&CS), based at Bletchley Park near London. Its original objectives were to help break the complex Enigma communications code used by the Germans and to transmit disinformation. The second organization was the Special Operations Executive

(SOE), founded in 1940 to carry out sabotage behind enemy lines and provide assistance to resistance groups operating in countries occupied, or controlled, by Germany.

After World War II ended, a new type of conflict called the Cold War began. On one side were the U.S. and its allies, including Great Britain. On the other side were the Soviet Union and its allies in Eastern Europe. During the Cold War, the SIS joined with the CIA in a number of operations to undermine the KGB, the main Soviet intelligence agency. For example, during the 1960s, SIS agents managed to recruit several important KGB

EVOLUTION OF ESPIONAGE
Bond, Sidney Bond?

Some people believe that British super-spy Sidney Reilly was a model for Ian Fleming's James Bond. Handsome and fearless, Reilly loved adventure. He began spying for Great Britain in the 1890s. Once, during World War I, Reilly parachuted behind German lines, posed as a German worker, and gathered secret information at a German arms factory. He killed two guards as he escaped back to England. After the war, Reilly became determined to overthrow the new communist leaders in the Soviet Union. He traveled in and out of Russia, posing as a member of the Soviet secret police, until one trip in 1925, when he was arrested and executed.

operatives as double agents. At the same time, though, it was discovered that key MI6 leaders had been selling British and American secrets to the Soviets.

Budgets for Britain's spy work were severely slashed during the 1970s, and the agencies shrank in size. Then Margaret Thatcher was elected prime minister in 1979 and made espionage an important part of her foreign policy throughout the next decade. The staffs of both the SIS and MI5 were expanded to include more than 2,000 employees each during that time. That is believed to be the current staff size, although exact numbers are still kept under wraps.

Since the end of the Cold War and breakup of the Soviet Union in 1991, the SIS and MI5 have concentrated on combating terrorism, particularly at home and in the Middle East. British espionage efforts have been directed toward uncovering the secrets related to wars in such places as Kuwait and Iraq and to bombing attacks such as those made on the London public transit system in 2005. These new types of threats have required British intelligence agencies to update and retool their methods of spying for the 21st century.

EVOLUTION OF ESPIONAGE
Breaking the Code

Solving the Enigma was one of the greatest cryptographic feats of all time. The Enigma was a German code machine used during World War II. It was capable of producing 150 quadrillion different combinations of letters and numbers to substitute for the actual letters in a message. A group of 10,000 code-breakers working at the SIS's Government Code and Cypher School at Bletchley Park took on the Enigma. The code-breakers designed a seven-foot-tall (2 m) machine called the "Bombe" that could decipher thousands of codes per minute, including those produced by the Enigma. Unlocking the Germans' secret messages gave the British a decisive advantage against their enemy.

German soldiers encrypted messages using the Enigma code on machines while in the field.

WORKING FOR THE FIRM

Do you have what it takes to be a spy for the SIS? Take a quick inventory of your skills, appearance, and personality. If you're a fan of James Bond movies, you probably think you need to be great-looking, daring, and a little conceited. Not surprisingly, the movies exaggerate reality. SIS agents *are* expected to be smart, resourceful, and self-reliant like Agent 007. But they are not required to be as attractive or as unconventional. In fact, the SIS would rather hire average-looking people who can blend in with others around them, as the best spies are those who don't stand out in a crowd.

What are some other ways that novels and movies exaggerate spy work? For one thing, very few SIS employees spend their time breaking into impenetrable fortresses and engaging in hand-to-hand combat. In fact, only a small percentage of SIS operatives actually do undercover spy work themselves. The agency calls these individuals "case officers." They are the people who are often

stationed in foreign countries, where they gather intelligence vital to British political and economic interests. According to the SIS's Web site (www.sis.gov.uk), case officers "have ... the ability to read others and influence their decision-making." They need to be persuasive—and even a little underhanded when situations call for it—to convince others to spy and run the risk of being caught and punished. Sometimes that requires appealing to someone else's ego by flattery. At other times, it may call for using blackmail. Some case officers may get to use top-secret

tools and weapons to collect information or to carry out covert actions. Most, however, spend their time recruiting others in the countries where they are stationed to do the undercover work. They take on the role of handler.

Assisting the case officers abroad or in Great Britain are two other types of SIS employees: targeting officers and reports officers. Targeting officers need to have excellent organizational and analytical skills. They are the people who help plan the operations and direct much of what the case officers do. They get their title from the way they keep everything moving smoothly and "on target." For example, they might help select

Opposite: Actor Daniel Craig made his James Bond debut in 2006's *Casino Royale*.

EVOLUTION OF ESPIONAGE
Taking Risks

One of the Allies' secret weapons during World War II was an organization of civilian volunteers who risked their lives in German-occupied Europe. The organization was the British-run Special Operations Executive (SOE). SOE operatives usually parachuted into enemy territory late at night or arrived secretly by submarine or small boat. Then they began their work, which involved spying, sabotaging Germans, and supporting resistance fighters. Many SOE agents were caught by the Germans, and their punishment usually involved torture or execution. Between 1940 and 1944, 393 SOE operatives were sent into occupied France. Of the nearly 120 captured, only 17 survived.

the individuals whom case officers should recruit to do undercover work. They might also pick out locations for drops and convey the intelligence that has been gathered to officials at headquarters.

Reports officers are experts on different countries and different subjects. They perform a lot of research and write many reports as a result, which explains their title. They are responsible for distributing intelligence reports from the field to government leaders who need to know the information, and they often represent the SIS at meetings with other government organizations on specific topics. Reports officers spend most of their time in Britain, even when their minds are traveling to foreign locales.

To survive in the field, an SIS case officer needs a good legend, or cover story. The legend answers the questions *Who am I?* and *What am I doing here?* Some case officers work under their own names. In spy talk, they are legals— they do their spying and recruitment while officially working in the British embassy in a foreign country or in a British-owned business. If they are caught breaking the foreign country's law, they are usually sent back to England rather than jailed.

Other case officers are classified as illegals—they work under a false name and a made-up identity. Sometimes their cover stories are very intricate. For example, the SIS may create a fake business in which some employees are illegals. The business serves as a front for collecting intelligence and relaying it back to Great Britain. If illegals are exposed as spies, they often

Opposite: Paratroopers (those who are dropped by parachutes from aircraft) have to practice how to land.

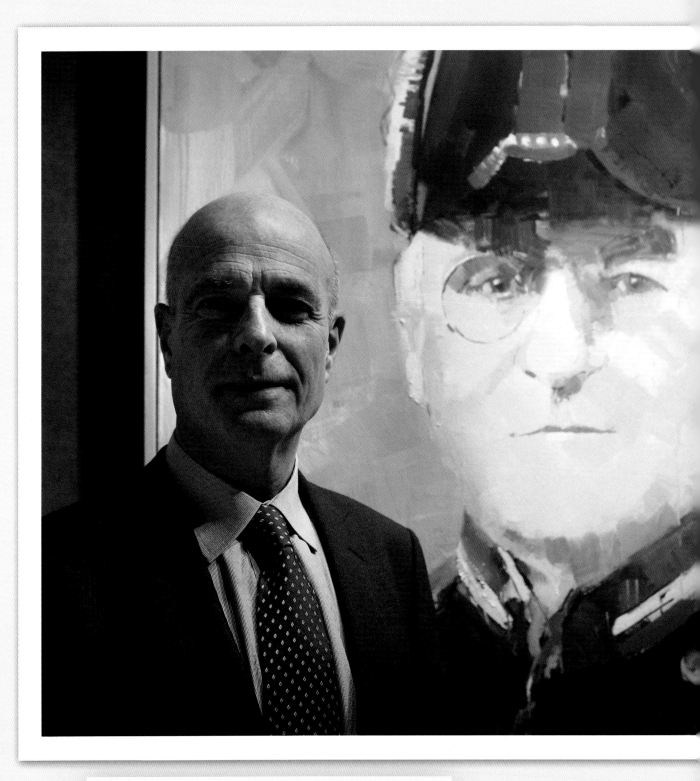

Above: Sir John Scarlett, SIS chief from 2004 to 2009, in front of a painting of the agency's first chief, Mansfield Cumming.

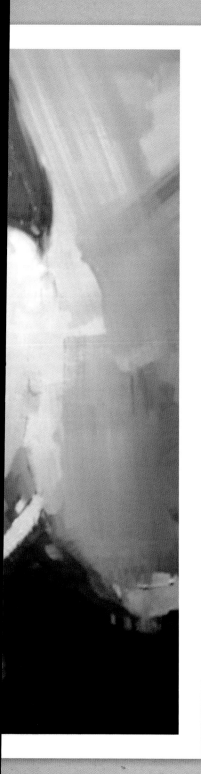

face stiff prison sentences.

What makes people want to be spies—or agree to become spies, even against their will? The reasons vary as to why British citizens choose to become case officers. Some are looking for adventure; others may want to serve their country. The work is challenging and constantly changing, yet it is often dangerous. "It is also quite glamorous," said one SIS agent who was interviewed on a British radio program. "You might find yourself on one day in … a tent talking to … tribal leaders in the middle of nowhere and 24 hours later be in a different country talking to a high-powered financier."

Citizens of other countries may have different explanations for why they spy for the SIS. Some do it because they are paid well for the information they uncover and transmit. Others work for the SIS because they feel their home country's government is oppressive or because they have a strong belief in the ideals represented by Great Britain and its allies. Others may be blackmailed into spying to cover up secret or illegal activities they have engaged in. Those who think that their wits and courage would best be suited for spying may be drawn to the SIS as well.

In the past, SIS agents were often recruited from major British universities such as Oxford. They were literally tapped on the shoulder by someone connected to the agency who believed they would make good additions to the Firm. Today, the SIS does its recruiting via the Internet or by advertising with universities. There is even an online exam that potential recruits can take. One activity involves a test of memory to see whether the recruit will be able to establish a cover and remember the details well enough not to slip up under questioning.

Recruiting is followed by several tough interviews and then a thorough security check. If a potential agent gets that far, the serious training begins and can last for 6 to 18 months. Case officers going into the field need to learn tradecraft. These skills include developing a cover and improvising on it as the need arises; spotting a tail and avoiding being followed; using spy cameras, radios and radio detecting devices, and other communication tools; mingling comfortably at parties and in the streets; coordinating secret meetings to recruit local assets; and setting up a drop for collecting intelligence from assets. Then recruits are ready to begin their careers as spies and become immersed in a world of secrecy.

TACTICAL MATTERS

In the 007 movies, James Bond may be the hero, and "M" may be the boss, but the real stars are the amazing gadgets and weapons created by the SIS technical staff led by an officer known as "Q." Whether Bond is driving around in a car that can transform into a plane or submarine, firing nerve gas from a fountain pen, or microfilming secret documents with a camera concealed in a watch, viewers are dazzled by an assortment of spy technology. While most of these gadgets are only movie props, real-life SIS agents have had some incredible tools at their disposal created by the agency's technology division.

Many of the gadgets developed by SIS technicians are designed to be held in the hands of agents or concealed on their bodies or in their clothing. They fall under the category of HUMINT, or human intelligence, tools, because it takes a human to operate such gadgets and collect or transmit data with them. Two examples that were developed for British agents during World War II

were a matchbox with a tiny camera hidden inside and a shaving brush with a secret compartment for storing messages or rolls of microfilm. A more modern hand-held gadget is a watch with a built-in digital tape recorder. An agent can call in to the watch with a cell phone to receive a playback of the recording. Other HUMINT tools employed by case officers include night-vision goggles for investigating in the darkness, tiny bugs for eavesdropping on conversations or secret meetings, and miniature cameras hidden in tie clasps or jacket buttons.

In his controversial book

The Big Breach, former SIS agent Richard Tomlinson describes several gadgets and communication techniques he was taught to use during his training. One device employed a short-range agent communication (SRAC) system. It allowed an agent to convey brief messages directly to a handler inside a British embassy or other approved location without making face-to-face contact or even sending an electronic communication, cutting down on the risk of interception. According to Tomlinson, here is how the SRAC system worked: "The agent writes a message on a

Spy cameras of the 1950s were about the size of today's digital point-and-shoot cameras.

HUMINT tools such as night-vision goggles can be used for missions that require stealth.

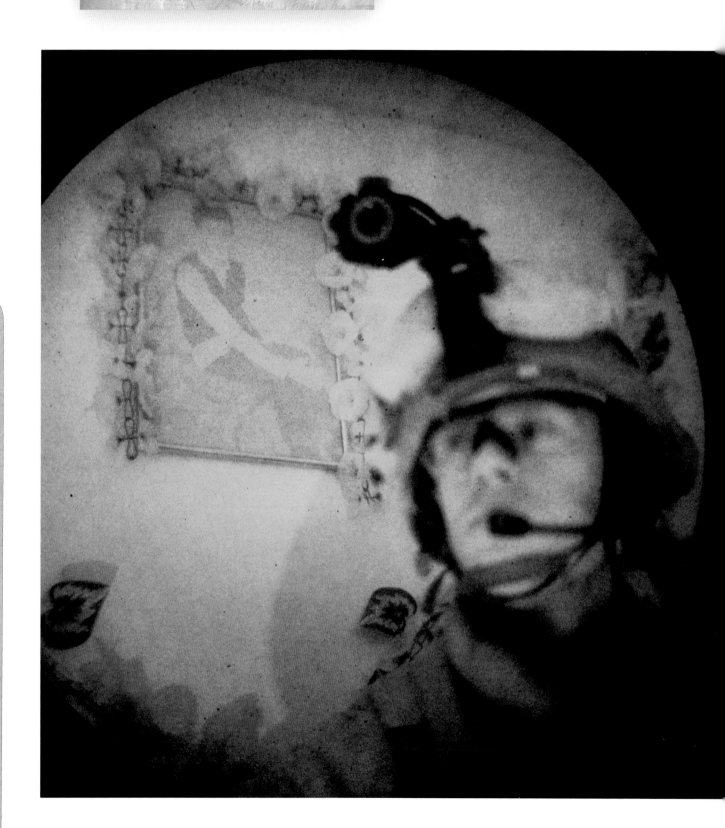

James Bond's cars were specially equipped to help the agent avoid being captured.

laptop computer, then downloads it into the SRAC transmitter, a small box the size of a cigarette packet. The receiver is usually mounted in the British embassy and continually sends out a low-power interrogation signal. When the agent is close enough, in his car or on foot, his transmitter is triggered and transmits the message [which has been converted into high-frequency radio waves]. The transmitter is disguised as an innocuous object, and for many years 'Garfield Cat' stuffed animals were popular as their sucker feet allowed the agent to stick the transmitter on the side window of his car, giving an extra clear signal as he drove past the embassy."

Tomlinson's training also focused on using special photography tools. "We were taught … how to take long-range snaps of targets using huge telephoto lenses and how to take clear close-ups of documents," Tomlinson said. They also practiced "with gadgets such as midget cameras and specially made collapsible document-copying cameras. Best fun, though, were the lessons on covert photography during which we secretly photographed members of the public with a variety of still and video cameras mounted in briefcases or shoulder bags."

In today's spy world, HUMINT gadgets such as the ones Tomlinson learned to use have

taken a back seat to ELINT (electronic intelligence), SIGINT (signal intelligence), and PHOTINT (photographic intelligence) tools. ELINT tools are used for computer monitoring and hacking; SIGINT tools are used for intercepting radio, telephone, and other communications; and PHOTINT tools are used for studying photographs taken by spy planes, satellites, or human operatives. All of these new methods fall under the heading of TECHINT (technical intelligence).

For modern spies, learning to use electronic gadgets has become an important part of their tradecraft. Far less significant is knowing how to handle weapons. In fact, unlike James Bond, many SIS officers seldom use guns, knives, or rocket launchers in their work. Today, it is probably more important for a spy to know how to hack into a computer than how to engage in hand-to-hand combat. Computers can be bugged with a keystroke recorder that can help an agent determine a user's password

59 L 354.
57c J 14. 15. 19. 20
30. 1. 18 . 1.

British agents have used PHOTINT since photography's beginnings, including during World War I.

and duplicate any commands that were previously typed in. Other software, or computer programs, can be installed to enable an agent to download files for later analysis. Most information today is stored and sent digitally, so knowing how to unlock digital files enables a case officer to uncover enemy secrets and, perhaps, foil their plots.

Backing up SIS agents in the use of TECHINT is another British intelligence agency. Known as the Government Communications Headquarters (GCHQ), it was established after World War II as a successor to the GC&CS that broke Germany's Enigma codes. GCHQ carries out many of the same functions as the National Security Agency (NSA) in the U.S. Its 5,500 employees use technology to intercept and interpret electronic communications and develop intelligence to combat terrorism and crime in Great Britain.

GCHQ also supplies intelligence to British military forces and to SIS agents around the world. Its data is often shared with foreign intelligence agencies such as the CIA as well.

In an example of cooperative intelligence work, in September 2010, operatives from the SIS and GCHQ, working with CIA agents, used TECHINT tools to thwart a plan to bomb London and several other European capitals. The plot was being developed by terrorists based in England and Pakistan. Intercepted e-mail and phone conversations—as well as aerial reconnaissance of terrorist training facilities in Pakistan—helped reveal the plot. British and American leaders decided to take action quickly. Several unmanned CIA drones flew over parts of northwestern Pakistan, firing missiles to destroy vehicles in which terrorists were riding. Taking out the leaders helped suspend the threat, but European capitals remained on high alert for several days following the drone attack.

Opposite: All sectors of Britain's security services monitor the daily movements of the country's citizens.

SUPER—AND SURPRISING—SPIES

Movies and novels usually portray British spies as dashing, well-mannered, and maybe even a little bit stuffy. The country's real-life spies have often been very different, and some of their stories may seem surprising. Take John Dee, for example. Dee was an astrologer and mathematician who lived in the 1500s. He was adept at reading people's horoscopes. When Queen Elizabeth I assumed the English throne in 1558, she called on Dee to help choose the best day for her coronation. Soon, she began consulting Dee on various matters, and he became her personal spy in the court. Dee signed his secret letters to the queen with a symbol made up of two circles and a bracket that resembled the number seven. Some historians believe that the symbol represented a pair of eyeglasses on a handle and that Dee was indicating that he was serving as the queen's eyes. Others say Dee was the original 007, some 400 years before James Bond made his first appearance in an Ian Fleming novel.

Another seemingly atypical British spy was Robert Baden-Powell, who is best known as the founder of the Scouting Movement (from which the Boy and Girl Scouts organizations came). In the 1890s, Baden-Powell served as an army intelligence officer reporting on Austria-Hungary, one of Great Britain's enemies at the time. While on assignment, he demonstrated that he was a great actor as well as a spy. One time, Baden-Powell dressed up as a nearsighted butterfly expert exploring the countryside. He made sketch after sketch of insects, adding images of enemy fortifications in the background. These he relayed to British military leaders in the region. On another occasion, Baden-Powell pretended to be a drunken fisherman boating along the Danube River. In that disguise, he was never questioned as to why he was sailing so close to a key Austro-Hungarian fortress. The enemy soldiers even showed Baden-Powell how to operate a new machine gun they were testing.

Several successful British authors have also doubled as spies for the SIS, mostly in wartime.

Opposite: Double agent George Blake escaped from prison (and his 42-year sentence) in 1966.

EVOLUTION OF ESPIONAGE
Double Agents

In the 1950s, the SIS's reputation suffered several serious blows. In 1951, reports linking two British Foreign Office leaders to a Soviet spy ring were leaked. Even worse, the reports hinted that the operatives' friend Kim Philby, who was in line to become the next SIS chief, might be a Soviet spy as well. All three men eventually escaped to Moscow before they could be arrested. Starting in 1953, another agent, George Blake, also began spying for the Soviets in East Berlin. He was finally caught in 1961, but not before he had revealed key British intelligence secrets to his new bosses.

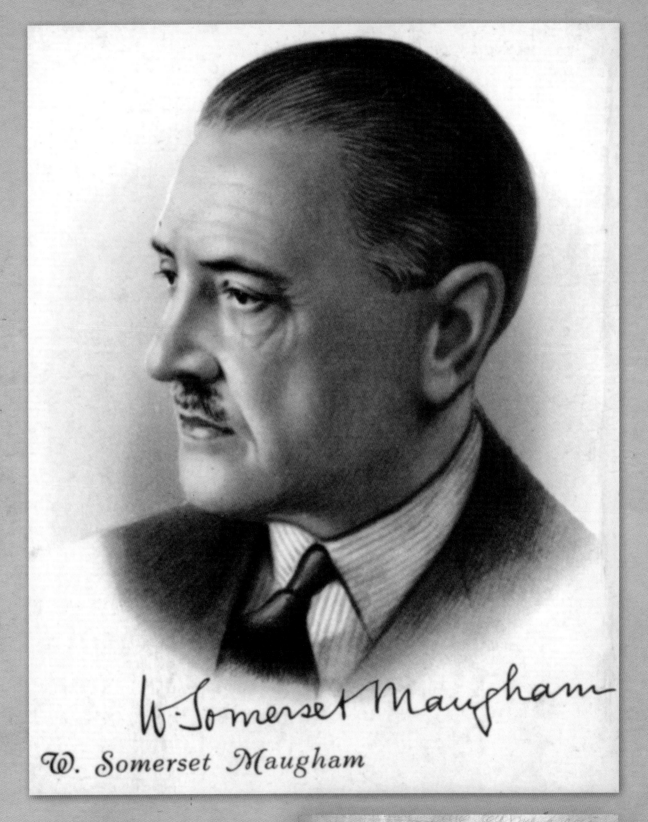

W. Somerset Maugham

W. Somerset Maugham

Maugham was recruited by British intelligence while serving as an ambulance driver in World War I.

Below: Dahl's embassy work helped him meet many famous Americans and publish his first children's stories.

British spymasters reasoned that the well-known writers would not raise enemy suspicions if they appeared in strategic places in Europe, Asia, or Africa. During World War I, novelist W. Somerset Maugham did intelligence work in Europe and was even sent into Russia soon after the 1917 revolution. He was tasked with trying to prevent the communists from making a separate peace with the Germans that would enable Germany to concentrate its troops in the west, in countries such as France and Belgium. After the war, Maugham wrote a collection of stories entitled *Ashenden* based on his intelligence work. Before the collection was published, however, he burned several stories that might have violated the Official Secrets Act.

Another literary spy was children's writer Roald Dahl, later known for books such as *James and the Giant Peach* and *Matilda*. After a plane crash that grounded the Royal Air Force pilot with serious injuries, Dahl was assigned to the British Embassy in Washington, D.C. His diplomatic position became a good cover as he worked to keep U.S. leaders interested in helping European nations win World War II and recover after it was over.

Dahl's boss in the U.S. was William Stephenson, a true intelligence mastermind. British prime minister Winston Churchill personally sent the Canadian-born Stephenson to America in 1940 with a dual mission: to keep an eye on German intelligence operations in the U.S. and to oversee covert operations aimed at getting the U.S. to enter the war by whatever means necessary. In 1940, the U.S. was still a neutral country, and many Americans opposed becoming involved in what they thought was Europe's war. This attitude was known as isolationism.

Stephenson set up an office in midtown New York, established a radio link with London, and chose his new code name, Intrepid. Then he set to work undermining the isolationists. He started by recruiting American journalists, authors, advertising copywriters, and artists to join his operation, which became known as the British Security Coordination (BSC). At one time, several hundred

Americans were part of the BSC. The journalists helped Stephenson plant stories in newspapers or on the radio to cast the isolationists in a negative light. Well-known authors such as mystery writer Rex Stout wrote pamphlets, and top copywriters created ads that emphasized the evil activities of the Nazis. The pamphlets and ads revealed other secret Nazi "plans" (all untrue) to set up training camps in Mexico for an eventual invasion of the U.S. and even to replace crosses on European churches with swastikas, the Nazi symbol. Stephenson's propaganda campaign began to sway American opinion. Still, it was not until the Japanese attacked American ships at Pearl Harbor on December 7, 1941, that the U.S. officially joined the Allies in the fight against the Germans and Japanese.

After Stephenson's main objective was successfully completed, he remained in America to run a much smaller SIS station throughout the rest of the war. He also helped his close friend William Donovan establish a civilian intelligence agency in the U.S. called the Office of Strategic Services (OSS). That agency would later evolve into the CIA.

The SIS kept busy during the

EVOLUTION OF ESPIONAGE
War at the Bottom of the World

The SIS was nearly caught napping in 1982 when troops from Argentina invaded the Falkland Islands off the southern coast of South America. Great Britain controlled the Falklands, but Argentina believed it should own them. When the Argentines staged their invasion on April 2, British intelligence officers were surprised. They had not detected any warning signs beforehand. Still, the SIS jumped into action quickly. With the help of French intelligence agents, who provided the SIS with plans for the French-built aircraft and missiles that had been purchased by Argentina, SIS operatives were able to sabotage many weapons and bring the conflict to an end.

British forces did not escape the Falklands War unscathed, losing ships such as the HMS *Antelope*.

Cold War, primarily working to turn Soviet agents into double agents or plant moles inside communist intelligence agencies in Russia and other Eastern European countries. One of the most important of these double agents was Oleg Gordievsky, an officer with the KGB, the Russian equivalent of the SIS. In 1973, Gordievsky approached SIS agents and offered to provide them with information about KGB activities and plans. He met more than 150 times with SIS contacts, who took more than 6,000 pages of notes on

what proved to be accurate intel. Gordievsky also alerted the SIS to the presence of several traitors operating inside the agency.

Less than two years later, Gordievsky was himself betrayed by a CIA officer named Aldrich Ames, who was a mole for the Russians. Gordievsky was recalled to the Soviet Union and feared he would be executed. However, SIS agents helped him defect to Great Britain. In the 1980s, he served as an adviser to British prime minister Margaret Thatcher and American president Ronald Reagan.

SPY TALES

During the 20th and 21st centuries, the SIS and other British intelligence agencies have been involved in some amazing spy missions against a wide range of enemies—from Germany and its allies during World Wars I and II to Middle Eastern terrorists in the 2000s. Some missions have been great successes, while others have been embarrassing failures.

As World War I broke out in 1914, both the SIS and MI5 mobilized to discover any German spies working in England. Most active spies were captured quickly. An example of this involved a pair of Dutch spies posing as cigar importers in England. They would telegraph orders for cigars, with the product type and number of boxes ordered representing the number of different types of ships they saw coming into British ports. Suspicious of the large number of cigars being ordered, British agents arrested the pair, who were later executed for their crime.

One of the most extensive intelligence operations during World War II involved the founding, supplying, and directing of the SOE between 1940 and 1945. The SOE was made up of civilians, or people not belonging to the military, who worked in Nazi-occupied countries such as France, Belgium, Poland, and the Netherlands. In defining its mission, the SOE appropriated a quote from Winston Churchill: "You are to set Europe ablaze!"

SOE operatives were covertly dropped behind enemy lines, where they set up equipment workshops and radio systems. They sabotaged transportation and power lines, disrupted enemy communications, and destroyed factories supplying arms and equipment for the enemy. SOE agents may not have set Europe on fire, but their efforts did make German military oficers boiling angry.

Many of the 3,000 SOE operatives were women without any previous military or intelligence experience, such as Odette Sansom and Violette Szabo. Sansom was born in France and moved to England after marrying a British man. In 1942, she volunteered to return to France as a

Opposite: Violette and Etienne Szabo got married less than two months after meeting each other in 1940.

radio operator for the SOE. Around the same time, Szabo, whose husband had been killed in action in North Africa, also joined the SOE. Both women were later captured by the Germans, tortured (though neither gave up any information), and imprisoned with many other people in concentration camps. Sansom survived the war, but Szabo was executed.

No spy operation during the 20th century was more dramatic or extensive than Operation Bodyguard, the plan to deceive Hitler and the German generals concerning when and where the Allies would invade Europe in 1944. Allied military leaders had already decided to invade at Normandy in northwestern France around June 6, a date known as "D-Day." The objective of Operation Bodyguard was to persuade the Germans that the invasion would come later and at a different location, such as Pas de Calais, several hundred miles east of Normandy. The operation took its name from another quote by Churchill: "In wartime, truth is so precious that she should always be attended by a bodyguard of lies."

Starting in late 1943, British and American intelligence groups began feeding lies to the Nazi intelligence agency, the Abwehr. Double agents working for the SIS sent reports to Germany about troop buildups in southeastern England. Fake press releases about fictional military units began appearing in magazines and newspapers. A prisoner swap was arranged to return a dying German general to his homeland. First, however, the general was driven past a military camp where he saw hundreds of planes, tanks, and tents. The general was told that they were traveling through Sussex, but they were really in Dorset several hundred miles farther west. The Germans became convinced that Pas de Calais was the target, and Hitler directed most of his troops there instead of Normandy. When the Allies struck on D-Day, casualties were great but not nearly on the scale of what they might have been.

A decade later, during the Cold War, the SIS suffered through one of its most embarrassing operations. Known as Operation Stopwatch, the 1954 plan involved the construction of a tunnel beneath the Russian military

After the war, Odette Sansom married fellow SOE operative Peter Churchill in London.

The same year that "Legoland" (pictured) opened, MI5 moved its headquarters to Thames House.

headquarters in East Berlin to enable eavesdropping on phone conversations between East Berlin and Moscow. A similar tunnel had been built in Vienna in 1953, and valuable information had been recorded. There was a hitch in the plan for this new tunnel, however. The man responsible for taking notes at SIS planning meetings was veteran operative George Blake, who turned out to be a double agent working for the KGB. Over the next year, British technicians tapped hundreds of phone lines in East Berlin and recorded more than 400,000 conversations, many of which contained disinformation. Then, in 1956, the Russians "accidentally" discovered the tunnel while doing repair work below their building and shut it down. It would

be many years before the SIS learned of Blake's treachery.

During and following the Cold War, the SIS worked closely with the CIA on several vital operations. In 1962, for example, the U.S. was involved in a confrontation with the Soviet Union over Soviet weapons being set up in Cuba, a communist island nation just 90 miles (145 km) from Florida's southern coast. Many people feared that a nuclear war—using weapons of unprecedented destructive power—would erupt. Information supplied by the SIS, courtesy of a double agent named Oleg Penkovsky, convinced the Americans that the Russian weapons were not as powerful as they had originally feared. President John F. Kennedy stood up to Soviet premier Nikita Khrushchev,

EVOLUTION OF ESPIONAGE
Legoland

In 1994, the SIS officially opened its new headquarters in London. Located along the river Thames in southwestern London near Vauxhall Bridge, the building has a unique shape and lots of nicknames. Some SIS employees called it "Legoland" because it looks as if thousands of the toy blocks were used to assemble it. Others call it "Babylon-on-Thames" because it seems to resemble an ancient Babylonian temple. No one outside SIS is sure just what special features the building includes, as such details are top secret. It is rumored, though, that a tunnel under the Thames leads from Legoland to British government offices in another part of the city.

EVOLUTION OF ESPIONAGE
Plot against Saddam

In 2003, the U.S. and Great Britain fought together to topple Iraqi dictator Saddam Hussein. That was not the first time that a joint American-British team had sought to overthrow Hussein. In the late 1990s, agents from the CIA and SIS tried to convince a group of unhappy Iraqi military and intelligence officers to stage a revolt against Hussein. The Iraqi leader's own intelligence forces discovered the plot, however, and he ordered at least 80 conspirators to be killed and hundreds more arrested. The CIA and SIS chiefs were doubly angry—both that the revolt had been planned without their approval and that it had failed so completely.

demanding that the Soviets remove their missiles, and the Soviets backed down.

The SIS and CIA have remained close allies into the 2000s. Prior to the American-led invasion of Iraq and the toppling of Iraqi leader Saddam Hussein in 2003, SIS reports on Iraq's military strength and possible possession of chemical and biological weapons were a factor in president George W. Bush's decision to call for the invasion. Such weapons were never discovered, but the British stood by the Americans throughout the war, providing military and intelligence assistance. Similarly, the CIA has consulted with the SIS in key operations designed to combat terrorists, such as those related to the 2005 London transit bombings and later threats of attack both in Europe and the U.S.

While Great Britain's military and political might in the world has declined in the past century, the innovative nature and scope of its intelligence work have remained strong. The spy agency of James Bond and Mansfield Cumming continues to be involved in exciting missions, both fictitious and factual, and the work of its agents remains vital to world security in the 21st century and beyond. As the agency notes on its Web site, the SIS prides itself on the ability of its employees to make a difference in the real world.

Opposite: The "7/7" attacks in London in 2005 prompted copycat attempts later that month.

ENDNOTES

aerial reconnaissance–spying activities conducted through the air using airplanes, balloons, and drones

agents–people who work for, but are not necessarily officially employed by, an intelligence service

Allies–the side in World War II that included the United States, Great Britain, France, and the Soviet Union

assets–hidden sources acting as spies or providing secret information to a spy

astrology–the study of how the movements and positions of celestial bodies affect life on Earth

bugs–electronic listening devices that usually contain a microphone, transmitter, and antenna

Cold War–the hostile competition between the United States and its allies against the Soviet Union and its allies that began at the end of World War II and lasted until the collapse of the Soviet Union in 1991

communist–describing a political and economic system in which all goods and property are owned by the state and shared by all members of the public

covert operations–undercover or hidden activities

cryptographic–related to the art of writing and deciphering messages in code

cypher (or cipher)–a type of code in which numbers and/or letters are substituted for regular text in a system to keep messages secret

decipher–to break secret codes, or ciphers, often used to send spy communications

defect–in the context of spying, to choose to leave the control of one country's intelligence service to work for another country; defectors often provide vital information to their new country

disinformation–false or misleading intelligence, often provided by double agents

double agents–spies for one country who double as spies for a second country and often provide false information to the first country

drones–unmanned aircraft, often directed by remote control, that are used to take secret photographs of or attack targets

drops–secure locations that usually include a sealed container where spies and their handlers can exchange information or intelligence materials to avoid meeting in person

embassy–the headquarters of an ambassador and staff in a foreign country

handler–a case officer who is responsible for recruiting and directing agents and assets working in a country

intelligence–information uncovered and transmitted by a spy

moles–employees of one intelligence service who actually work for another service or who work undercover in a foreign country in order to supply intelligence

operative–an undercover agent working for an intelligence agency

propaganda–material distributed to promote a government's or group's point of view or to damage an opposing point of view; some propaganda is untrue or unfairly exaggerated

resistance groups–organized underground movements in a country fighting against a foreign power that is occupying the country

tail–someone following a spy who is acting undercover

tradecraft–the procedures, techniques, and devices used by spies to carry out their activities

WEB SITES

Bletchley Park: The Machines
http://www.bletchleypark.org.uk/content/machines.rhtm
Find out more about famous cipher machines from Britain's National Codes Center.

MI6 Opens Its Secret Archives
http://news.bbc.co.uk/today/hi/today/newsid_9018000/9018456.stm
Listen to an interview with historian Keith Jeffery about MI6's early years.

SELECTED BIBLIOGRAPHY

Coleman, Janet Wyman. *Secrets, Lies, Gizmos, and Spies: A History of Spies and Espionage.* New York: Abrams Books for Young Readers, 2006.

Crowdy, Terry. *The Enemy Within: A History of Espionage.* Oxford: Osprey Publishing, 2006.

Dorril, Stephen. *MI6: Inside the Covert World of Her Majesty's Secret Intelligence Service.* New York: Free Press, 2000.

Jeffery, Keith. *The Secret History of MI6.* New York: Penguin Press, 2010.

Owen, David. *Spies: The Undercover World of Secrets, Gadgets, and Lies.* Buffalo, N.Y.: Firefly Books, 2004.

Thomas, Gordon. S*ecret Wars: One Hundred Years of British Intelligence inside MI5 and MI6.* New York: Thomas Dunne Books, 2009.

Tomlinson, Richard. *The Big Breach: From Top Secret to Maximum Security.* Moscow: Narodny Variant Publishers, 2000.

Volkman, Ernest. *Spies: The Secret Agents Who Changed the Course of History.* New York: John Wiley & Sons, 1994.

INDEX